21st Century Skills Library

GLOBAL PERSPECTIVES

TERRORISM

Robert Green

Cherry Lake Publishing
Ann Arbor, Michigan

CHERRY LAKE Publishing

Published in the United States of America by Cherry Lake Publishing
Ann Arbor, Michigan
www.cherrylakepublishing.com

Content Adviser: Melinda K. Redman, Senior Director of Intelligence and Analysis, Terrorism Research Center/Total Intelligence Solutions

Photo Credits: Cover and page 1, © Ramzi Hachicho, used under license from Shutterstock, Inc.; page 4, © Bruno Pagnanelli, used under license from Shutterstock, Inc.; page 6, © Stocktrek Images/Alamy; page 7, © Crispin Rodwell/Alamy; page 9, © JUPITERIMAGES/Brand X/Alamy; page 11, © Andrew Fox/Alamy; page 13, © ArkReligion.com/Alamy; page 15, © Reuters/Corbis; page 17, © Natalia Bratslavsky, used under license from Shutterstock, Inc.; page 18, © Dominic Burke/Alamy; page 20, © JUPITERIMAGES/Thinkstock/Alamy; page 22, © Richard Levine/Alamy; page 24, © Steve Skjold/Alamy; page 26, © Sally and Richard Greenhill/Alamy

Map by XNR Productions Inc.

Library of Congress Cataloging-in-Publication Data
Green, Robert, 1969–
Terrorism / by Robert Green.
p. cm.—(Global perspectives)
Includes index.
ISBN-13: 978-1-60279-125-1
ISBN-10: 1-60279-125-2
1. Terrorism—United States—Juvenile literature. I. Title. II. Series.
HV6432.G734 2008
363.325—dc22 2007038920

Cherry Lake Publishing would like to acknowledge the work of The Partnership for 21st Century Skills. Please visit www.21stcenturyskills.org *for more information.*

TABLE OF CONTENTS

CHAPTER ONE

A Peaceful Refuge

Afghanistan has a history of conflict, including struggles against terrorism.

Sidiq Massoud, a young boy from the country of Afghanistan, could not believe the peacefulness of Interlaken, Switzerland. He marveled at the quiet streets of the sleepy resort town nestled in the mountains. He had come to Interlaken, however, not as a tourist, but to take part in an international student conference on global issues. On the first day of the conference, he found himself chatting with a young girl from Northern Ireland named Megan Sweeney.

"I hope that Afghanistan will be this peaceful one day," Sidiq said to Megan. "Afghanistan also has many mountains, but they have not seen such calm in a long time. For most of my life, there has been fighting in Afghanistan. But at least we have driven out **al Qaeda**."

"Do you mean the people who attacked the United States?" asked Megan, still struggling with the Arabic name of the world's most well-known **terrorist** organization. "I still don't know what they were trying to do."

"Before 9/11, we had no idea what al Qaeda was," said Johnny Chen, a boy from New York who was representing the United States at the conference. "Today, preventing another attack is a major concern for Americans."

Sidiq had seen many American soldiers in Afghanistan. The U.S. military invaded Afghanistan after 9/11 because the leaders of that attack had used his country as a base for their terrorist operations.

"Yes," said Sidiq, "you came to know the same terror that we lived with in Afghanistan. Our government at the time allowed these men to use

A U.S. soldier walks up a hill in Afghanistan to check caves for terrorists.

Afghanistan to plan attacks in other countries. We are glad that al Qaeda has been driven out."

As delegates to the International Global Issues Conference, Sidiq, Johnny, and Megan hoped to find some answers. They had been assigned to a group studying **terrorism**, especially the war on terror. They hoped to learn exactly what terrorism was and what they could do about it.

Air travel makes it easy for people and goods to move around the world.

★★★

The increasing travel of goods and people between nations is commonly known as **globalization**. Globalization has many aspects that are positive and some that are negative. One of the negative results of globalization is the ease with which global terrorist organizations can strike at people far away from their own homes.

On September 11, 2001, terrorists **hijacked**, or illegally took control of, four commercial airliners. The terrorists flew two of the planes into the Twin Towers of the World Trade Center in New York City. One other plane crashed into the Pentagon, the office building that houses the highest-ranking U.S. military personnel. The last plane crashed into a field in Pennsylvania after the passengers struggled with the terrorists. The events of that day are commonly referred to as September 11 or 9/11, and it made terrorism one of the most important global issues of our time.

The U.S. invasion of Afghanistan was just one part of the war on terrorism that resulted from the 9/11 attacks. The war on terror has become a global event, with countries around the world becoming involved.

Life & Career Skills

Everyone has opinions, and other people will not always agree with them. Reaching agreements between people with different opinions and different objectives is the core of **diplomacy**. It takes the ability to see things from other people's point of view and to compromise. Diplomacy is the main avenue for communication on global issues between governments. Good diplomats need good public speaking skills and good listening skills. They must be able to argue their positions and listen carefully to the arguments of others.

CHAPTER TWO

What Makes a Terrorist?

The Twin Towers of the World Trade Center in New York City were destroyed by terrorists on September 11, 2001.

"So are terrorists people who belong to al Qaeda?" asked Johnny.

"They are terrorists," said Megan, "but there are other groups of terrorists all over the world fighting for different things. It is important to

Learning & Innovation Skills

Most people agree that terrorism is the use of violence, or the threat of violence, to achieve a political or social goal. Terrorists use violence to create fear and get publicity for their cause. In the process, people are hurt and property is destroyed. Take a look at each of the actions on the list below. Do you consider it a terrorist act? Why or why not?

- threatening someone with violence
- kidnapping
- killing a government leader
- phoning in a bomb threat
- bombing a building
- hijacking an airplane

realize that terrorists generally do not call themselves terrorists. They are usually fighting for something that they believe in."

"In England, we have had attacks by Irish terrorists," said James Brudenell, a young man from London.

"But many believe that the British have no right to be in Ireland," said Megan, angrily. She was referring to the British control of Northern Ireland, which some people in Ireland oppose. "You can be against the British in Northern Ireland and not be a terrorist."

"Yes, but if you blow up a bomb in London, then you are a terrorist," said James.

"I get it," said Johnny. "Terrorism refers to using certain types of violence against innocent people."

"Yes," said Megan. "It's not really a question of what those people believe in, but whether or not they attack innocent people. It's the type of behavior that matters, like blowing up a building or an airplane with innocent people in it."

Muslim children at an Islamic school read the Koran, the holy book of Islam.

"And many **Muslims** in the Middle East are not happy about certain policies of the United States government," said Sidiq. "But only terrorists would attack the United States, like they did on 9/11. Just remember that very few Muslims are terrorists, and Muslims like myself do not consider these terrorists to be Muslims at all."

★ ★ ★

Muslims are people who follow the religion of **Islam**. This religion started in Saudi Arabia and spread all over the world. Today, there are many countries where most of the people are Muslim, especially in the Middle East. Most people in Afghanistan are Muslims. But some **extremist** Muslims use their religion as an excuse to use violence to promote their political views.

The war on terror is a war against Islamic terrorists, those who want to spread a form of **radical** Islam through violent attacks. These terrorists say they are fighting for Islam, but most Muslims disagree with them.

Though they claim to be religious warriors, Islamic terrorists are politically motivated. They use violence, like the 9/11 attacks, to make a political statement. Al Qaeda planned the 9/11 attacks in an effort to get the U.S. military out of Saudi Arabia and other parts of the Middle East.

Islamic terrorists also believe that religion should guide the political life of nations. They see Western countries and especially the United States as dangerous for Muslims. They argue that these countries influence Middle Eastern governments for their own benefit.

The government of Saudi Arabia, for example, is a close ally of the United States. Saudi Arabia has large supplies of oil, which Americans rely on to drive their cars. Saudi Arabia also supplies common products like fertilizers, plastics, and jet fuel. This is an economic relationship that is very important to the United States. But Saudi Arabia is also the place where Islam began. Two cities in the western part of the country, Mecca

Crowds of Muslims gather to pray in the holy city of Mecca.

and Medina, are holy cities to which Muslims travel to honor and celebrate their religion.

Osama bin Laden, the leader of al Qaeda, is from a large, prosperous family in Saudi Arabia. But he opposes the relationship between the United States and Saudi Arabia. He thinks that Saudi Arabia should be a

Learning & Innovation Skills

In the United States and most countries of the world, religious life is separate from the government. The reason is that not all people hold the same religious beliefs. Separating church and state (religion and politics) is intended to protect the rights of different religious groups. If church and state are kept separate, no religious group can use government programs to limit other religious groups.

Not everyone agrees with this way of thinking. In countries such as Iran, religion still plays a major role in political life. Islamic extremists also want religion to play a central role in government. Why do you think Islamic terrorists want to keep religion and politics connected? What role do you think religion should play in public life?

more Islamic state, based on religion, and that there should be no cooperation with the United States or other non-Muslim countries. His views, therefore, are both religious and political. He is an enemy of both the United States and Saudi Arabia, which his group has also attacked.

★ ★ ★

"So by using terrorism, al Qaeda can spread their political views and make people in the United States and Saudi Arabia afraid," said Johnny.

"Yes," said Sidiq. "Unfortunately, terrorists are helped by the amount of news reporting that follows a terrorist attack. Of course, news reporters should cover such a big story, but the coverage allows the terrorists to have a voice all over the world."

CHAPTER THREE

A New Kind of War

A group of Taliban fighters travels on a road in Afghanistan in 2001.

"How do you fight against people who move around like terrorists do?" asked Megan. "They move from one place to another. It's not like war used to be."

"That is why it is a global problem," said Sidiq. "In Afghanistan, terrorists could operate freely because of the country's weak government. Eventually, we had to drive out our own government and start a new one that would fight against the terrorists."

The war on terror is a new kind of war. Traditionally, wars are fought between different countries. They use armies, and there are rules, such as trying to avoid hurting **civilians**, or people who are not in the army. But terrorists do not have a country. They travel from one place to another to avoid being captured. They use the Internet to communicate and to spread their message. They pose a threat to people everywhere.

To fight terrorism, the United States under President George W. Bush adopted a new strategy. In the past, terrorists were hunted by using **intelligence agencies**, which tried to secretly spy on them to determine where they were and what they planned to do. President Bush declared that his country would use the army to attack terrorist groups.

That is what happened in Afghanistan. The government had been taken over by a group of radical religious extremists known as the **Taliban**. They let al Qaeda use Afghanistan to plan attacks in other countries. People in Afghanistan were scared of both the Taliban and al Qaeda.

Before attacking Afghanistan, the United States appealed to other countries for support and approval. It is a big step to send troops into someone else's country. But after 9/11, most nations believed that the United States should invade Afghanistan and drive out al Qaeda and the Taliban. The United Nations, which tries to bring about cooperation between different countries, voted to support the U.S. invasion.

The flags of many nations fly in front of the United Nations building in New York City.

The invasion was largely successful. Afghanistan established a new government that the people could participate in, and al Qaeda was driven out of the country. But some terrorists escaped and crossed over the border into neighboring Pakistan and to other countries. This illustrates one of the difficulties of stopping terrorism. Terrorists may be driven out of one country, but they find a place to hide and continue operations in another.

Protestors in London demonstrate against the war in Iraq in 2005.

Some people don't agree with this new kind of war against terrorism. They wonder who should decide what countries should be invaded. After the invasion of Afghanistan, the United States invaded Iraq. Many people opposed the U.S. invasion of Iraq, and the United Nations did not support it. Many countries said that Iraq had no connection with the terrorists, but U.S. government leaders believed it did. Today, U.S. troops are still in Iraq. Terrorists arrived in Iraq after the U.S. troops invaded, to fight Americans. But the invasion made people in many Middle Eastern and African countries worried. Would they be next? Would the United States keep invading Muslim countries?

Today, people around the world debate how to fight terrorism. Even in the United States, many politicians and scholars argue that the war on terrorism should rely less on military invasion. They say that using intelligence agencies to spy on terrorists and cooperating with foreign governments to arrest them is a more effective policy. This approach would make greater use of international policing and of diplomacy, the official communication between governments.

The problem with relying on diplomacy is that most countries do not want to negotiate with terrorists. Since the terrorists are not part of any government, they do not follow international law. This makes it extremely hard to use diplomacy to solve the problem of terrorism. So, although many Muslims opposed the U.S. invasion of Iraq, they believe that strong measures should be used to fight against terrorism wherever it exists.

21st Century Content

Terrorists communicate using the Internet. They set up their own Web sites to convince more people to join them. Law enforcement and intelligence agencies, such as the Federal Bureau of Investigation and the Central Intelligence Agency in the United States, need computer experts to monitor the terrorists' online activities to find out what they are up to. If you are good at using computers and gathering information on the Internet, you are building the skills needed to do these kinds of jobs.

CHAPTER FOUR

Living in a Changed World

Department of Homeland Security employees help keep U.S. airports safe by screening passengers and baggage.

"How has the war changed life in the United States?" asked Sidiq.

"Well, many things have changed," said Johnny, trying to think back to life in the United States before 9/11. "Not only have U.S. policies changed to combat terrorism, but even the government has been reorganized."

Johnny was referring to the creation of an entirely new branch of the federal government, the Department of Homeland Security. Before the creation of this department, protecting the United States from a terrorist attack was the duty of people in many different agencies, or parts of the government.

"What about the Patriot Act?" said Megan. "I have heard it's very controversial. How do Americans feel about it?"

"Well, some people think it is a good idea, and some people are worried about it," said Johnny. "You have to remember that legal protections for individuals are very important to people in the United States. These are known as civil liberties."

The Department of Homeland Security, established in 2002, coordinates the efforts of various agencies that work to protect the United States from another terrorist attack. The department helps secure seaports where ships bring in goods from other countries. It helps secure airports where many people enter the United States every day. This government agency also coordinates information from the Central Intelligence Agency and the Federal Bureau of Investigation. It shares this information with local law enforcement officers and others working to prevent terrorist activity.

A man holds a sign at a protest against the Patriot Act.

The Patriot Act, passed in 2001 by Congress, the lawmaking branch of the U.S. government, makes it easier for government officials to take a closer look at people's lives to see if they pose a threat to the United States. The act provides additional powers for the government to gather information by listening to phone conversations, reading e-mail, and investigating financial transactions and bank accounts.

According to its supporters, the Patriot Act allows investigators to catch terrorists faster and possibly save American lives. But others worry that this law makes it too easy for the government to investigate innocent Americans. They argue that it limits the **civil rights** of U.S. citizens in a way that makes people uncomfortable.

Since 9/11, life hasn't just changed for people in Afghanistan, Iraq, and the United States. Leaders all over the world have tightened security at their country's airports and seaports. There is also greater cooperation between intelligence agencies, which share information about terrorist activities. People all over the globe have become much more concerned about terrorism. Terrorists travel in planes, trains, and boats like anyone else. They use the Internet to communicate. That means they can plan attacks from almost anywhere. This realization has changed life for people almost everywhere.

Life & Career Skills

After the terrorist attacks on September 11, 2001, people in the United States became worried about Muslims living in the United States. People wondered if they were friendly or if they were sympathetic to terrorists. Islam is growing quickly in the United States because of Muslim immigrants who move to the United States and because of converts, or people who adopt Islam as their new religion. Most Muslims are patriotic Americans, just like Christians or Jews.

Do you want to know more about Muslims and their faith? Talk to Muslims directly and visit their mosques. Like other religious groups, they usually welcome visitors. Most Muslim groups in the United States encourage people to learn about their religion and the daily life of Muslims.

CHAPTER FIVE

What Can We Do?

An instructor teaches a group of teenagers how to perform CPR. Learning first aid and CPR will help you to be prepared for emergencies.

After a week of talking about the war on terrorism, the students thought they had a pretty good understanding of what terrorism was.

"But what on earth can we do about it?" said Megan. "It's such a big problem."

"The U.S. government says that kids, like adults, should be prepared to help prevent another terrorist attack," said Johnny. "They say that you should notify an adult if there is something suspicious or if you see a package sitting by itself in a busy place. They recommend that you learn first aid so you can help if people are injured. You should also know how to contact law enforcement or emergency personnel."

★ ★ ★

Governments are trying to get people involved in alerting law enforcement officials if they know when a dangerous event is about to happen. They are also interested in keeping people calm if there is an emergency. They would like people to be able to help each other in the event of a terrorist attack.

While these are responses to the threat, these strategies do not address the root causes of terrorism. One thing that scholars agree on is that people who join terrorist organizations feel like they don't have an outlet for their political views. This is partly because governments in places such as Saudi Arabia and Egypt do not allow people to fully participate in their government. People therefore feel frustrated.

That frustration is made worse by poverty. When people don't have good jobs or a safe living environment, they are more likely to do desperate things, such as turn to violence. This is called a developmental view of terrorism. According to this theory, helping other countries economically and politically will reduce the number of people who are drawn to terrorism.

There is no question that there is a lot of misunderstanding between Muslims and people in Western countries today. It is important to realize that most Muslims are peaceful and that they believe terrorists are criminals.

A Muslim brother and sister prepare a meal to be shared with the poor. It is important to remember that most Muslims are peaceful people.

The war on terror will not be fought just on a battlefield. It is a much more complicated fight. It is a war of ideas, fought on many fronts including on the Internet, through mass media, and with **propaganda**. It requires people from all over the world and especially in the Muslim world to cooperate with each other to isolate the terrorists. This kind of cooperation can only happen if we have a better understanding of people from other cultures and are open to communicating with them.

★ ★ ★

"People from many countries are helping to open schools, build roads, and facilitate trade in Afghanistan," said Sidiq. "This will give us a better chance to keep the Afghan people directed away from violent groups. But it would also help if people understood our religion better. Many Muslims feel like the West is against them, because we want a different kind of society."

"So you mean that even in peaceful Interlaken," said Megan, "we are helping a little bit to understand each other?"

"I think you understand much more about Afghanistan after this week than you did before," said Sidiq. "And I understand much more about the way you think and your opinions. I can't help thinking that this is a good place to start."

21st Century Content

Intelligence agents secretly record conversations that terrorists have on their telephones. This is one of the main jobs of a spy agency like the Central Intelligence Agency. These conversations are often described as "chatter," growing talk about an attack or a new development in a terrorist group. To understand that chatter, intelligence agencies hire language experts. These experts translate the conversations from a foreign language into English so that they can determine if it is important. Once the chatter is translated, experts put all of the pieces together to try to find connections between groups. They want to be able to find terrorists before they have a chance to carry out any planned attacks. Besides foreign language skills, what kinds of skills do you think an intelligence agent needs to be successful?

CENTRAL AMERICA AND WEST INDIES

ARCTIC OCEAN
GREENLAND (Denmark)
SVALBARD (Norway)
Arctic Circle
ICELAND
See inset below
RUSSIA
ASIA
EUROPE
KAZAKHSTAN
MONGOLIA
GEORGIA
UZBEKISTAN
KYRGYZSTAN
TAJIKISTAN
TURKMENISTAN
ARMENIA
TURKEY
AZERBAIJAN
NORTH KOREA
SOUTH KOREA
JAPAN
CHINA
PACIFIC OCEAN
AZORES (Portugal)
CANARY ISLANDS (Spain)
MOROCCO
TUNISIA
LEBANON
SYRIA
IRAQ
IRAN
AFGHANISTAN
KUWAIT
BAHRAIN
QATAR
PAKISTAN
BHUTAN
NEPAL
ISRAEL
JORDAN
ALGERIA
LIBYA
EGYPT
SAUDI ARABIA
UNITED ARAB EMIRATES
BANGLADESH
INDIA
LAOS
TAIWAN
Tropic of Cancer
WESTERN SAHARA (Morocco)
MAURITANIA
CAPE VERDE
MALI
NIGER
CHAD
SUDAN
ERITREA
YEMEN
OMAN
MYANMAR (BURMA)
THAILAND
VIETNAM
PHILIPPINES
NORTHERN MARIANA ISLANDS (United States)
WAKE ISLAND (United States)
GUAM (United States)
MARSHALL ISLANDS
SENEGAL
GAMB.
GUINEA
BURKINA FASO
BENIN
AFRICA
DJIBOUTI
GUINEA-BISSAU
GHANA
NIGERIA
CENTRAL AFRICAN REP.
ETHIOPIA
SRI LANKA
CAMBODIA
BRUNEI
MALAYSIA
PALAU
FEDERATED STATES OF MICRONESIA
SIERRA LEONE
LIBERIA
CÔTE D'IVOIRE
TOGO
CAMEROON
SOMALIA
MALDIVES
KIRIBATI
UGANDA
KENYA
RWANDA
Equator
SAO TOME AND PRINCIPE
GABON
EQUATORIAL GUINEA
DEM. REP. OF THE CONGO
BURUNDI
TANZANIA
NAURU
INDONESIA
PAPUA NEW GUINEA
SOLOMON ISLANDS
TUVALU
CONGO
SEYCHELLES
COMOROS
INDIAN OCEAN
EAST TIMOR
ATLANTIC OCEAN
ANGOLA
ZAMBIA
MALAWI
MADAGASCAR
NAMIBIA
ZIMBABWE
BOTSWANA
MAURITIUS
VANUATU
FIJI ISLANDS
Tropic of Capricorn
REUNION (France)
AUSTRALIA
MOZAMBIQUE
NEW CALEDONIA (France)
N
W
E
S
SOUTH AFRICA
SWAZILAND
LESOTHO
FRENCH SOUTHERN & ANTARCTIC LANDS (France)
NEW ZEALAND
SOUTH GEORGIA & SOUTH SANDWICH ISLANDS (U.K.)
Antarctic Circle
ANTARCTICA
EUROPE
NORWAY
SWEDEN
FINLAND
RUSSIA
ESTONIA
North Sea
DENMARK
Baltic Sea
LATVIA
LITHUANIA
RUSSIA
IRELAND
UNITED KINGDOM
0 400 mi
0 400 km
BELARUS
NETH.
POLAND
BELG.
GERMANY
ATLANTIC OCEAN
LUX.
CZECH REPUBLIC
UKRAINE
LIECH.
SLOVAKIA
FRANCE
MOLDOVA
SWITZ.
AUSTRIA
HUNGARY
SLOVENIA
ROMANIA
MONACO
SAN MARINO
CROATIA
BOS. & HERZ.
SERBIA
Black Sea
GEORGIA
ANDORRA
PORTUGAL
SPAIN
ITALY
MON.
MACEDONIA
BULGARIA
ALBANIA
GREECE
TURKEY
GIBRALTAR (U.K.)
MOROCCO
ALGERIA
TUNISIA
MALTA
Mediterranean Sea
CYPRUS
SYRIA
LEBANON

Glossary

al Qaeda (ol KYE-duh) the Arabic name for the terrorist organization led by Osama bin Laden; in Arabic, it means "the base" and has inspired many other terrorist groups

civil rights (SIV-il RITES) the fundamental protections people have by right of being a citizen of a country; in the United States, these rights are outlined in the Constitution and by laws passed by Congress

civilians (si-VIL-yuhnz) people who are not in the military

diplomacy (duh-PLOH-muh-see) the art of negotiating, especially between government leaders working on international agreements

extremist (ek-STREEM-uhst) a supporter of extreme political or religious views

globalization (GLOHB-uhl-i-ZAY-shuhn) the growing interconnectedness of people in different countries, especially economically and politically

hijacked (HYE-jakd) something taken over by force, such as an airplane or ship

intelligence agencies (in-TEL-uh-juhnss A-juhn-seez) government organizations that collect and analyze information on possible national threats, often through spying

Islam (i-SLAHM) a religion that believes in the god Allah, whose prophet is Muhammad; Islam began in Saudi Arabia and spread throughout the Middle East and to many other parts of the world

Muslims (MUHZ-luhmz) believers in the religion of Islam

propaganda (prop-uh-GAN-duh) information that is spread to try to influence the way people think about an issue or to damage the reputation of those with different viewpoints

radical (RAH-dih-kuhl) a person who holds extreme political or religious beliefs, often considered dangerous

Taliban (TAL-ih-ban) a fundamentalist Muslim group that ruled Afghanistan from 1995 until the U.S. invasion in 2001

terrorism (TEHR-ur-iz-uhm) the use of violent acts against nonmilitary persons to create fear and achieve political goals

terrorist (TEHR-ur-ist) a person who uses terrorism to achieve political goals

For More Information

Books

Baker, David. *CIA & FBI*. Vero Beach, FL: Rourke Publishing, 2006.

Baker, David. *Department of Homeland Security*. Vero Beach, FL: Rourke Publishing, 2006.

Freedman, Jeri. *America Debates Civil Liberties and Terrorism*. New York: Rosen Central, 2008.

Web Sites

The Department of Homeland Security

www.dhs.gov/index.shtm

Find out what measures are being taken to protect the United States and its citizens

FEMA for Kids—National Security Emergencies

www.fema.gov/kids/nse

Learn about the precautions to take during a time of a national security emergency

Global Incident Map

www.globalincidentmap.com/home.php

View an interactive map showing locations of terrorist threats, risks, and incidents

Index

About the Author

Robert Green has written more than 30 books for students. He is a regular contributor to publications on East Asia by the Economist Intelligence Unit and holds graduate degrees from New York University and Harvard University.